6⁹⁵

For Nancy,

the conscience

of the shop.

Keep 'em honest.

Best,
Rick
Sept '88
Houston

A Breakthrough Book
No. 57

THESE MODERN NIGHTS

Poems by
Richard Lyons

Richard Lyons

University of Missouri Press
Columbia, 1988

Copyright © 1988 by Richard Lyons
University of Missouri Press, Columbia, Missouri 65211
Printed and bound in the United States of America

Library of Congress Cataloging-in-Publication Data
Lyons, Richard.
    These modern nights : poems / by Richard Lyons.
        p. cm.—(A Breakthrough book ; no. 57)
    ISBN 0-8262-0672-7 (alk. paper)
    I. Title. II. Series.
PS3562.Y4494T4   1988   87-26355
811'.54—dc19   CIP

The publication of this book has been supported by a grant
from the National Endowment for the Arts.

∞™ This paper meets the minimum requirements of the
American National Standard for Permanence of Paper for
Printed Library Materials, Z39.48, 1984.

In memory of my mother
& for my father
& for BTB

The Devins Award for Poetry

These Modern Nights is the 1989 winner of The
Devins Award for Poetry, an annual award
originally made possible by the generosity of
Dr. and Mrs. Edward A. Devins of Kansas City,
Missouri. Dr. Devins was President of the
Kansas City Jewish Community Center and a
patron of the Center's American Poets Series.
Upon the death of Dr. Devins in 1974, his son,
Dr. George Devins, acted to continue the Award.

Nomination for the Award is made by the
University of Missouri Press from those poetry
manuscripts selected by the Press for
publication in a given year.

Acknowledgments

Acknowledgment is made to the following publications where some of these poems appeared, sometimes in earlier versions: *The Antioch Review* ("Home"); *Crazy Horse* ("The Umbrella," "So Swiftly Past," and "Hands"); *The Denver Quarterly* ("A Season"); *The Indiana Review* ("These Modern Nights"); *Ironwood* ("Summer Vacations" and "Near"); *The Nation* ("Burning Stars"); *The New England Review* ("Land's End"); *The New Republic* ("Chichikov's Driver"); *Poetry* ("Constellation"); *Shenandoah* ("The Doctor & The Young Groom"). Parts of a poem entitled "Chiemsee" *(The Nation)* have been incorporated into "These Modern Nights," section 10.

The author would like to thank the people at Inprint, Inc., The Criterion Fellowship, and The Stella Ehrhardt Memorial-Cullen Fellowship for their generous support, as well as William Olsen, David Wojahn, Michael Bowden, and Michael Milburn for their faithful attention to these poems.

The epigraph to this collection is from *The Selected Works of Cesare Pavese*, trans. R. W. Flint (Farrar, Straus, and Giroux, 1968).

"Hymn to the Sun"—Speaking of Bellini's *St. Francis in the Wilderness,* Sir Kenneth Clarke writes, "Here, at last, is a true illustration of St. Francis' hymn to the sun." From *Landscape into Art* (Harper & Row, 1976).

"Burning Stars"—Stanza 1 alludes to William Olsen's "Trees." The line "the Idle Star, the Strange Star, the Lowly Star" is taken from Olsen's "The Incarnations."

"These Modern Nights"—Section 6 takes a line from a song by the Talking Heads, Sire Records Company. Line from "Once in a Lifetime" by David Byrne, Brian Eno, Chris Frantz, Tina Weymouth, and Jerry Harrison is reprinted with permission, copyright 1980, Index Music Inc., EG Music Ltd., and Bleu Disque Music Co. Inc. All rights reserved.

"The Doctor & The Young Groom"—The epigraph to this poem is from *The Selected Letters of Anton Chekhov,* ed. Lillian Hellman (Farrar, Straus, and Giroux, 1984).

"The Umbrella"—The second line is from George Seferis's *A Poet's Journal: Days of 1945–1951,* trans. Athan Anagnostopoulos (The Belknap Press of Harvard University Press, 1974).

Contents

"These modern nights,"
Pieretto said, "they're as old as the world."

—Cesare Pavese

I

Near

The nets come up in the moonlight
empty-handed and faceless
as water is returned to water.
Once in a while
they get a fender or shopping cart.
A spike fish
puts its head up and smacks small waves back and forth
then goes back under.

Nothing knows or wants the prescience.
Not even the men whose business it is
want to find a face on the bottom of the river.
Children appear on the bridge, their heads
        the bull's eyes
oscillating under small moons.
One of them probably picked these dandelions
that flow by, going under.

Once in West Germany
I sat in the soapy water
and cried because nothing was familiar,
not even the chickadees in black masks
taking dips in the window box's icy water.

When I went swimming as a boy
I would dive beyond the useless cries
and sink until all the light, even the moonlight,
was left in the sky.
I would hear sounds
dropped inside cement blocks
like pears falling.
I listened to myself

and touched what I thought
were rocks and weeds
and once maybe a smallmouth
driven toward us by fishermen in chestwaders,
their nervous silver lures.

Maybe the fish wanted only to feed on algae
near the locks.

Maybe fear had nothing to do with it at all.
One of those nights my friends held me under
until I blew out a mouthful of air
and kicked deeper, further out:
a hole in the net of their arms
plain as mud over a windshield.
I rose toward their cries.
Michael and Jilly and a girl I didn't know.
Each body
the light of a star, a slow leak of air.

A Hymn to the Sun

As the Sisters lead us across the schoolyard
                beneath the soft cool olive trees,
the mourning doves coo from the shoulders
of stone women holding up the architecture

of their living quarters, what we call the Nuns' House
or the Convent—we say it fast

as if the women living there had ceased to live

                        to live in God,
thumbing bruised petals from the roses in their garden
where, once a year, on May Day, the bishop hears our sins.

He raises the hand with one bright strawberry, the ring
the nuns told us the Holy Father had blessed with water

                        from Palestine.
I remember that hand smelling like the tonic
barbers still slick across the back of my neck after a haircut.

                The bishop looks away,
clicking a cup of tea in a tiny white saucer.
His voice is soft, my penance an easy three Hail Marys—
this, long before I learn we're not absolved for anything,

                the nuns' "balance sheet"
held high above our heads by Saint Peter at the Gates,
an interminable series of numbers raised to an inscrutable
    power

                the way Trig means torture
nailing us above red-lined graph paper, a hive of symbols
        spilling from the lead point of a pencil.

As the bishop opens his eyes & draws the crucifix in the air,
I see a black-capped chickadee pinch a sunflower seed

from a plastic jug with its shoulder cut out.
It sways on a stiff brown string, then grows still.
This is the patience of Saint Francis of Assisi.

The bishop smiles, then lifts the thin stole
                            & kisses it.
It is the color of the sky when the weather is full
of the bad intentions birds sense when they flick away
from the gray shadow across a window.

As we run our fingers through the laminated *Lives of the
      Saints*
we grow older. Saint Theresa closes her eyes

to copper pennies, her body fainting inside the red-hot flame

                      of Christ,
that cruel color we reserve for the horns of Satan in the
      drawings
we enter in the Spring Art Fair.

                The beginning is
when John Malokowski takes first prize for a stark depiction
of wet black winter trees.

The beginning is when the Sisters lead us into their house,
the smell of incense & chicory—

                  the clean absence of men.

Like choir boys, our presence doesn't count.

The girls our age are ensconced in the Academy
on the other side of town.

            Sister Mary's face
is a blossom of undertaker's rouge, an ever-so-slight
              roseate dust across her cheeks.

We file in one by one, kneel & whisper fast automatic
          prayers.
My hand urges itself to touch the dead woman's curved
          smile.
I fear the thoughts inside my head are hers

                              or the devil's
or God's, the chaste way all our words abstract the earth.
After a while, each Sister lights a candle
                    with a long gray wick.
Each kneels & kisses the dead cheek.

Sister Helen, my brother's teacher, is sad,
the lines on her face remind me of the riverbeds
of Kenya in my geography book.

I want to remember her with another face: it's the day
my mother sends me to buy a Mass card for an uncle

                              I barely knew,
dollar bills looped around my index finger & stuffed in my
          trousers.

                    Arches
the color of sand lead me past the rectory, the chapel,
and the main church into the garden of the Sisters.
Sister Helen is lifting a finger from her huge black sleeves.

On the tip of her finger is a single sunflower seed.

                    A sparrow hovers,
whirling its wings fast through the air, its ruffled breast
          exposed.

In that moment I forget what, if anything, my mission is.

                    My body spreads
its wings as Sister turns & smiles.

                    Young man, she asks,
are you lost, why have you come?

Summer Vacations

The amusement park is empty,
"Out of Business" painted in red
on a big piece of pine leaning on a turnstile
                    we, as kids, shoved,
counting ourselves among the lucky,
                    vulnerable to rain, measles
and whooping cough: the limits of our small bodies.
We leaned beyond the Whip, the Tilt-A-Whirl,
beyond our deaths—as harried as the animals
dodging us for popcorn or the pink curl of cotton candy.

I remember the young giraffe's black tongue
like pumice rubbed on the palm of my hand, like the feel
of father's beard when he came home from work
and plopped in a chair, head back, eyes closed.

And I will always remember the llamas
suffering inside their straw-matted wool.
My brother Jimmy riding the glossy rump of a horse
on a Merry-Go-Round, which, to us, back then, moved

                    like the hands of the clock in school,
or the way the biplane, sputtering above the tilted beach
        umbrellas,
took forever to skywrite its fading letters of smoke:

ANIMAL FOREST PARK   OPEN YEAR ROUND.

                    By the time
I understood these hieroglyphics, they had disappeared
                    & reappeared many times
till the biplane's stuttering across the sky
was forgetful as the scudding shapeless clouds.

At fifteen a young beauty even my father called "a doll"
helped herd hot dogs over the fire.

                    Her name was Mary
like the purest girl in the Bible.

18

But the way my sisters talk—

      a two-month-old life

beneath her wedding gown,
I wonder if the albescent face I remember
is desperate & twisted now

      like a muscle sprain on an X-ray.

At fifteen she had a dupe.

For her, I wore chinos for the Sunball Dance. We didn't go.
I changed the same night into swim trunks.
We didn't go. I changed the same night into a turtleneck
so we might sit on the rocks above the gazebo

      & touch each other.

I no longer think of her with the obsessiveness
that makes memories glow

    like the iconographic representations of saints.

And Mary I'm sure doesn't think of me.
This is the equilibrium so celebrated these days,
a vague sort of loss that airbrushes each of us
out of any picture, leaving behind the place itself.

It's autumn, the fog weeping in off the waves

    like an alchemist's concoction,

seaweed driven up in serpent's-heads on the beach.

These could be the elongated bands of salt water taffy:
sea breeze, jamoca toffy, banana, mint.
For hours we watched them wind through the magical heart

      of the confectionery.

But it's gone or moved

    or I've got everything wrong.

My hand on the abraded bar of the turnstile,
I think of the cruel mirrors,
my sister's body like "the fat lady in the circus,"
what she had become from liquor & an uneasy marriage.

I remember my brother & I
as the Wild Mouse veered for the edge of the sky,
whipping back just in time to dip hard into the landing
        station
where a man drew back the bar & wished us good day
                of all the things he might have said.

In a cage a lion lies on his shelf
                like so many bags of groceries,
one crooked length of wood like a human elbow,
his paw like a winter muff tossed over the eyes.
I'm thinking: this is the end of love—
                        a shuffleboard disc
shoved so hard it skips up & bruises my father's shin.
I hear the waves open their white fists.
I hear the parrots & pink macaws.
The dark green trees gather each small lost breath
        against the infinite exactitude of time.

A Man Speaks

We do a job, it gets done, it wears a hole or two
in our cheeks and our hillsides
steep all year
so, like memory,
we forget the day as it gets dug as it forgets us
as it should. Our cars slide out of the lot
at the same time, after the whistle.
It's dark along the road
and we're thirsty. The Oasis has a light
that spiders the bar with light,
the charged turbine of music

and booze driving each of us into his own face
as the mouths of the cool mines
urge us down. Dusty coal and rock salt, as in a nagging
        dream,
are drawn up to the tune of ants
go marching one by one . . . a memory from childhood
moving out into air where things are dangerous.
Even the gravel comes up in the light
like eyeballs squinting not to take so much in,
screen door, girly magazines, beer, wrinkled shirts
blown off the line

the terrain a sleeplessness, a Sahara of hills.
As kids, we saved a long time
to see the flame eater's tongue cool the red coal,
to slip beneath tent ropes
and staging, the gray sky of an elephant's belly—
all to see the man's seared cheek,
his helplessness.
We saw an ash on his tongue.
All is faith, the life of earthworms
swallowed by the deepest light—a few beams of light
and pine between us and it.
Ten days of hauling and ten more

and my friend says he's about to do something crazy.
He pulverizes a mug to mica,
then his fist opens and two moths emerge.
Just another trick
like the deer etched on walls of niter
by teenagers.
Did we choose this vein of ore
crystallized so far below the earthworks
that boundaries heave and fall,
that pickaxes whet our names on stone,
our names on white stone
deeper, a little further down?

At the Window

Each mind drifts in and out of the evening.
In Wertmüller's *Seven Beauties*
a man surrounded by a blue fog
lifts a German Luger to his friend's head.
Later, he wakes screaming about the gigantic hams
of the commandant who swats him with her riding crop.
He can't abbreviate the past,
his friend's face in the rictus of the evening,
the dark spots on the hillside
that are cows, pigs, the letters P.O.W.
darkening in the particulars of rain.
The rest is circumstantial, the sisters
streetwalking, the gloss on their lips
washing off with the rain from their hair.

Sometimes what we say is love, a kind of desperate love,
is just the mystery and melancholy of the streets.
Each night is a freedom, a black reflection.
I lift the tone arm over a record,
the disc turning without sound below the stylus
like the cars passing in the rain-streaked windows:
an aquarium that doesn't invite us
or drive us away.
I remember a night with another woman, the row of flannel
        shirts
that weren't mine lined up in the closet.
The helpless way without a light
I had to crawl along the walls to the bathroom.
The breath on the lip of the water glass

tasted of tobacco and peppermint.
I was a minor character
shot early in the novel
to create gratuitous tension

or one just not mentioned after a while.
The night you left it was raining.
The lamp and the Zenith Portable
were dripping on the hood of the car.
You didn't say any more, the headlights curving.
In certain Middle Eastern countries, I remember,
when a woman leaves a man
he ties a beetle by a string to a nail
and draws a circle on the ground
like an arena.
As the beetle crawls round and round
shortening its tether
she eventually comes back to him.

2.

Water is running through the drainpipe
and the gutters.
A bottle is tossed from a speeding car.
On nights like these
we'd drive into Cambridge for a movie
with very little plot, subtitles
and a labyrinth of personalities.
Tonight I can't sleep or walk off the separations
sex becomes, an ache
to fascinate us with ourselves.
Hours pass, come tumbling out of these cupped hands
that touch nothing, and before I know,
it's light and I see the woman next door

standing on her porch,
breaking bubbles on the screen.
Then she comes out
inspecting the eaves of her house.
With her hand she stops the wind chimes
in the chinaberry
and feeds the birdhouse
three yellow biscuits.

Such splendid exactness!
It doesn't matter that it's summer,
that the cypresses along the avenue
press into the future.
Soon sailboats on the reservoir
will tack into a steady breeze

as she walks through her garden,
gathering strawberries in a demitasse
to surprise her husband
with the music their loss will make on his tongue.
Or maybe she'll want to make love
and afterwards they'll sit apart on the floor
like wrestlers breathing.
I'll write a letter,
read the newspaper.
The wind outside turns corners in the air
with a scrap of paper
as though I were the egress to a long and bitter meditation
and each of my neighbors
at the window, waiting, thoughtful,
pulled me through.

Burning Stars

Stick by stick, brickface
and foundation,
I've built this house, tacking down its hair.
And some nights, like this night, across the sky
a shooting star burns out
as we sit and watch it and want to know things.
Nothing conspiratorial tends toward us
except over Liquid Carbonic
the Idle Star, the Strange Star, the Lowly Star.
They all stick close
so far from us wind draws off their sticky
galactic scent.

Tonight out on the lawn
a carnival dragon filled with friends
shuffles its sequined spine of stars
and half-moons past storefronts
and alleys, each of us breathing the mothball
fire of its fabric and shouting louder
than the next, buffeting indignities
that can't change, that we are,
as meaningless chatter about work
allows the only real work
of memory—forgetting—to draw off into vapors
any evil personal enough to touch our lives
gathering again on the lawn
to say good-bye, the evening's over
when it's just begun, headlights curving
through the pepper tree and rhododendron.

Because I don't go away
I go upstairs
and place my hands like pink starfish on the window
and lower my head as if a slew of stars
were released in holding back
when the Hungry Star staggers in, intimate

as it expands my insides
where I don't live.
Will I be frightened enough to welcome it,
saying this pane of glass
is yours, you throb of light,
empty as the hullabaloo of stars is empty
even as I stand in it,
letting each of these prima donnas
touch me with its invisible dust.
As cruel and as generous
as the fire this one burns with,
let me drift separately,
a voice, a call deserted of voice.

Two Legs of the Same Journey

1.

Beef cows in a sea of beef cows
hem the car in, the cattle driver in shiny yellow chaps
cursing the lumbering meat *Daisy, Angel, Dingbat* . . .
the brick-brown hides we touch.
Later with a bottle of wine you grow closer to yourself
the way the evening closes in on us,
smaller for all the enlarging the dark has done
to arrive out of breath. Out of work, no wife,
you pop the fire with pine cones as mosquitoes whir
their broken-record song along the edge of everything,
the smell of Herefords and dust.

With a jack two Indian men pry the fender
off a wheel and listen to the blinking
voice on the cruiser's console
as a third, handcuffed a little drunk to the bumper
tells us they take the backroads down from Sedona
to the copper mines in the south
if the money's good and the pick-up turns over.

Later you and I uncurl sleeping bags
and listen to war cries for Pow-Wow, the hum
of generators on Winnebagoes, humpback whales
against the purple sky and shell of trees.
You draw yourself up in the remaining light
from road flares to say 'Mr. President, take me,
all the employment agencies
and public doles like soldering irons
count my teeth like cherished pieces
of mica found in the pocket
of all the unmentionable silences
I've moved away from, the small trees
and their misery. I am nothing you could
spit on with accuracy.

I am dust, fur, a ball of wax
in the ear of Justice who in her boredom
dreams of me, a lost American.
I am dust, did I say already
I am dust.'

2.

That's it: to empty yourself so completely
you can own some empty thing.
And night can go on quietly for once.
In the morning a waitress holds a baby
over the swirls of cream she pours in our coffee
as we look in, like the baby, not having shaken sleep off.
A daffy pelican dips its head in Cinzano
each time the barmaid drops a tip in its bill.
From the deck of the roadstand the clouds pale
and the mountains pay out to further mountains
like piles of rope as we ditch
this guy, this goner, *the farm dry*
as a fart the year she and the boy,
his mother tongue failing him
even now: a wife and small boy grown incandescent
in a fire that just might not be memory.
'You must love the details of my life'
the fire says,
'they love you.'

Chichikov's Driver

With the reins around his right hand, which is deformed,
an extra finger, he banks the horses through an opening in
  the trees.
The dew soaks his shoulder.

At the inn he smells a burnt taper snuffed out by another like
  himself.

The dead can be bought & sold. They dance on the rim of a
  coin
minted for the Czar. On the coin is a woman with a shock of
  wheat.

The horses splash their huge faces in the trough.

Above, at a window stands a woman who has been dreaming
  of a hand
with a moonstone on each finger, just a perfect detached
  hand.

Is this still her dream, a troika's black shape inside her hand?

She wants to drop a gown still warm with sleep down on the
  driver
nodding his head & chirping the names of the horses
as if they were his kids *Nikolai, Alexei, & Sasha.*

Hands

My mother & I are driving through the hills
of eastern Massachusetts where she's lived
all her life, some trees still dark
summer green though it's September
and the air is cool drawing down
on the sides of the car an angry blush
of sky diminished with the whoosh
we steer by or through to an exit ramp
curling between red autumn trees.

Behind a high white fence
cows low some, heads nodding.
They can be petted, urged on by kids
so the milk squeezed through farmers' fingers
drills a pail.
I touch lightly the brown hide of a calf,
a touch between baby velvet
and the sandpaper feel I'm told sharks' hides hold
long after they're hung up
in the Chinese fish markets.

Mother,
your words draw the rickety-legged
babe into air as though you exhaled
from within her the brew-breath cud
of yellow straw—*more* she seems to bawl
heading for the crib as the tip of her mother's
snotty mouth sends her down.
It seems a game, one the calf
can't understand & repeats.

2.

That day outside Reegan's drugstore
when I cussed out a station wagon
that cut us off

you reprimanded me
and I told you to drive your own fucking car home.
I was sixteen.
Later you forgave me for the words
my fourth-grade St. Vitus' Dance
shook out of me, for my shivering hand
that blurred the plastic windows
of model cars & British Spitfires,
for my shuddering chin & mouth pushing out
those words your mother washed out
with soap so Mary, God's Mother,
wouldn't sew your mouth shut.

Even then I knew this
as the darning needle's tale.
This mothership of summer insects
still draws on blond wings from the marsh
toward a boy pushing hamburgers & franks
across a grill. I wore a chef's hat
and kept franks from rolling off onto the ground
and when I didn't, shooing the beast,
I kissed them, dipped them by my sleeve & up to God,
stashing them back on the white-hot center.

3.

Ahead through a stand of elm
is a rock wall & beyond that, pumpkins strung out
on their pigtail vines.
We feel for the perfect face
of a jack-o'-lantern to frighten us
beyond frightening, now that day & night
are adult, empirical—like the peninsulas
and bays of black & white on the map
of a cow's side. The leaf shadows
put their hands on our faces
the way barely open blinds
let light touch us when we're alone
and humble & can't be held.

When I was born you prayed for my life
as the scalpel ran through the umbilical cord
wound around my newborn neck. Eight years later
you prayed for my hand to steady
long enough to grasp a hammer
or to peel the tiny colorful decals
from their backing to stick on the U.S.S. Arizona.
You taught me how to pray, fingertips
like a steeple or tent.
Your words calmed me
almost as easily as your long nails
lifted the insignia of a battleship,
the way my prayers—kneecaps
shaking on the floor—seemed to steady
the hand of the maple whirling outside
my bedroom window,
the way God must be easy, a leaf
thumbed with red from a tree
so we can press Him in a book
or miss Him, red-tipped, held & held by air.

A Season

There's a time when a child purrs on the hip
of its parent, a horse rubs
the old hickory
and the tree's bark splinters, cracks, not one drop of water,
no leaf.
Nothing falls, all is spent—

each whirl of wind dies & there's another
in its place. My father & I are talking money,
scum till you have it.
So I take it, bathe in it like grief, like soot
stinking up the birches along the Charles,
naa, naa, naa, every make of car.
Not one white tree.

That's why when we were six
we rode the branches down, the crack at the base
of the tree sounded like the crack of a bat
when Williams stood in.
When you're old enough
you want to stand still awhile,
not lose something each time you look.

You want to rub your father's arm
like a tarnished piece of silver,
tell him he's not looked at most things wrong
and that your fluted life never saved anyone.
You want to save his.

II

These Modern Nights

—to Paul

1.

In the yellow light she aims an iron around each button
on a blouse, like a woman in a study by Vermeer
sad or simply satisfied.

It's the bright blouse with the big lapels
she calls "Tropical Bird."

Outside, the hummingbirds tweak the nipple
of sugar, sweet dripping needle-nose
strings of light.

On a barstool
she swerves toward a man who shakes a rubber cup of dice
and thumps the bar.

This is your scenario.

The birds fly off.
An archangel glitters in a flash of cymbals
as the wah-wah pedal draws out each last

cold fret on the guitar.

2.

She drives out to the Stuckey's on the interstate
to drink coffee, to listen to the late-night cook
orchestrate his voice with the sear of meat,
a splash of onions on the grill.

The air is burnished, sinking in & out of itself.

The counter-boy's words are okay, like the salt
she nudges with a finger across the plate.

3.

Wrapped in a batter of dust
the hewn stone
muddies the water & leaves a trail of silt in the sink.

Drying on a wad of paper towels
the arrowhead dulls,
some childhood stone we'd imagined
Pocahontas strumming across a bowstring.

In this dream of childhood,
stunned, a deer kneels in a rut fed by thaw.
Its antlers shake
as if to get a hat on straight.

We snip off branches with a Swiss-Army knife
and suck the bitterness out,
mouth & eyes wincing.

Below, fog obscures the snowline:
hackmatack & fir.
We stood on the precipice
till things lifted & we could see the Protestant
and Catholic steeples
on either side of town,
the hydroelectric towers,
two billboards & the tops
of all the trees.

4.

This scenario is yours & is scenario
so nothing ends cleanly.

She's in the room not to talk to,
the smell of ironed clothes dry & sweet.

You've talked a marriage to death.
You know this & you're scared
and still you're talking, burrowing into the telling
—even her sighs scoff.

Your words are shadows. Cigarette smoke
pushes at the ceiling.

"I'm talking to you, Susan . . . "

"Am I the only one who hears me?"

5.

"She sees a guy who works at the Xerox place."

"I only saw him once from Quinn's, you know,
the frosted windows for seeing out
without being seen."

If you asked me
I'd gather her fingers in my own.

If you asked me I'd leave it alone.

Are you listening?

All I'm saying is the opaque look in her eyes
is the look of arrowheads we dug up as kids.

This doesn't make me any more generous of heart.
What do I know?

This doesn't make her the bone-white
statue of the Virgin.

6.

I lift over the lavender blue-black stain of loosestrife
along a bay where trawlers bring most everything up:
a serpent's-head of kelp, fish in flames, water
pouring out like muscles into water.

For now this scenario's mine, I guess.
We're ghosts sodden or sun-baked in our flesh.
Or I'm alone with a Pocket Larousse, tongue-tied & stupid
with only enough francs to haunt the bookstalls at
          Montmartre.
I stand beneath the stained glass of Saint Theresa
who burned with God's light, never again herself.

Aren't we all tourists counting the steps to Sacré Coeur,
naming the names, buying blood oranges off a cart?
Easels teeter on their brown stork legs
as women in yellow feather boas coo to passing taxis.

It's almost as my father said it would be, this story
of a woman who loves everyone, a few graceless moments
the scythe misses, gathering & scattering as it sings.
Combien, Combien. I hear its high-pitched tin
as every day back home you hear your neighbors
share their music, Talking Heads, The Clash,
This—is—not—my—beautiful—wife.
A child scrapes boundaries for hopscotch.
The night leans out & bellows.

7.

Beneath the dome hang the idyll, the hunt, the kill,
sex & sacrifice, all this in the past, a hushed trill,
as the Unicorn surrounds itself with "croquet-wickets."
Unlike us, it trusts so much reverence, doesn't it?

At the bubbler a boy slurps, then, arms out, swerves
too close to tapestries that set off alarms with a wave
of the hand. He might as well be the son you gave
to foster parents on the rich north shore, the same

puckered, unripe face we spied in Maternity
as he sped with others inside crystal star-pods
into another life, another name. He points, now, to the dome
where rain is tapping, says *la nuit, la pluie.*

The Unicorn's bemused smile grows miniature & mold-gray
inside the Virgin's hand-held mirror that looks like
the monstrance we daubed with linen for Father Dave.
Was it you saw the flame of Christ's brilliant eye?

The tiny oval outline of the face bleeds all others
even the pale tracery of sycamore in my wallet-photo:
Sox caps, spotted dog, our adolescent spines
curving away in the instant the camera clicked.

8.

At dawn as if through cheesecloth
I slip out of Paris.

From the train the curlicues of grape vines along the river
look like a child's first earnest try at his signature.

Near dawn, for three marks, I take a tour
of an underground city intended to push south
through the heart of the Alps.

Watch your step, the guide says, ninety-three steps.

At the bottom two dark eyes stare up,
two machine-gun emplacements.

Does my voice shiver at the chunks of concrete
torn away, the tunnel falling away
below the ground?
Winter ice seeps down from the surface.
What did I expect, some night cat unpinning his claws
point by point?

They say the farmers tore the place apart,
Hitler's bunker of ice.

I hunt my heart for the tiniest black chip.

9.

In Bad Wiessee & Boston
the children are ghosts.
They tingle against one another.
Light burns through them. A little girl
with her hair tied up on her head
like a model's, like Mommy's, scrapes a thin stone
on the pavement, boundaries to hop near
but never over.

An upstairs room begrudgingly gives up music:
the view of a hill falls away to firs
thick as beds of coal.
A horse lets one hoof fall
upon the boards.

It's your heart, Paul.

A little boy in fiery smock sits atop a fiery horse.
Come, his little hand curls,
but you do not.

10

At an outdoor café a man buys me schnapps
till my words slur, he wants someone
besides himself to lean into the clean
breeze off the Watzmann.
A fat boy is hosing the sidewalk.
The sidewalk is white & absolutely clear.
If the winds from the death camps
love the ash they so lovingly lift
it's the absence of thought, or the wings
of starlings, it's the soot from the chimneys
on the shoulders of the workers as they pass home
in the ding & clank of the trolley.

In spring they all go out to the forests
to ax branches dwarfed by memory.
On the backs of horses they drag fallen logs,
bark unraveling to powder.
But in the fairy tale one yellow-flecked
thief leaks each rosy teat
on the She-Goat—
then dips low through the shadows,
a drop of milk suspended from its beak.

If you ask me it's as though someone runs a hand
over a globe & when a teacher says Baton Rouge
he stops it with a finger
and says, there, I want to live there.
In the House of Puppets I overhear a boy say the sun
is throwing out all its little arms & legs—
what he calls the light across the blue
porcelain face of a doll. He says he's a rocket
and pointing to his sister: "you're a telephone."
It's natural sometimes to forget you, Paul.
I walk past a hock shop selling sabers, war medals—
the road an iron-gray strand of hair
on the pillow of a dead man sleeping everywhere.

11.

From my desk
in a kindergarten classroom where I teach the rules
to pilots & M.P.'s, I stare out on rock-face
and over the low-pitched roofs that stud the mountainside
like bits of chocolate. Carved out
of green construction paper & pasted on white
by Bavarian schoolchildren, the alphabet
stares too, a sort of stupid marvel,
blackboards as shiny as the wings of grackles.
Sometimes in the middle of what I'm saying
I'll turn & see a boy, always the same boy,
through the window.

His hair is a splash of mustard or a daub of yellow
or it's the halo rising off the mist of a mountain lake.

The boy is running & calling back to his sister,
a yellow dress.
If she were a sunflower she'd soon glare down on
the marigold cheeks of her stern German brother.
I could believe that this Hansel & Gretel
pushed an old woman into an oven
then turned & turned, eyes closed,
till the wide-eyed children of fable
unfurled, unfurling from foil
some gingerbread stashed in the notch of a tree.
Don't you remember, Paul, the white wolves we were
curled up in our snow den.
We collapsed the door
till our breathing hurt.

Once we ran through a field of dry grass,
thrashing sticks, Sinbad or General Custer.
No crickets, not a peep, or some single
silent fool on the tip of a blade of grass—
cumbersome as a gunboat.

We cut him down,
standing in the middle of that fear & quiet.

Now I live where palm fronds clash in wind.
From some Erect-A-Set
a boat-tailed grackle rises
to squirt over the grass
with his gawky tail.
I know you can't hear me, Paul.
This long travelogue falls inward
like a snow fort.

I see the Canada geese, Plum Island.
It's 1981.
When they stand still
the little ones
are scruffy brownish clumps of grass.
Expecting them all to lift,
you raise your hands
for that unbelievable creaking of wings,
twilight the color of mop water
muddier & muddier till black.

Some rise in their own good time
on drafts of ocean air,
flailing wings on the water's edge
to scare off whitetail deer.
I know, I know, I play back the past.
I vault myself over the hollow sound of my steps
on the swampwalk.
I sink in the sluggish surf of sand
—you & the dog already small figures up the beach.
I'd like to be something more than a speck
in the late period of sand
but each time I play this back it loses something,
like the Tavel we uncorked & tossed down
making separation celebratory, never dulled by use.
Your father would dress a bird, mallard or blue teal,
with an old blade that wore clean through.
We'd chase a few with rubber-tipped arrows

—but that sort of manliness seems odd to me now,
what we spent a long time becoming.

I'm speaking to you from another edge,
a marsh in Texas
where alligators roll in the unrippling
seep of tide.
I'd like to say that for me it's Plum Island, 1981,
you and the dog small & sure.
Out on the yellow disc of the water
a fisherman is talking to his line,
it goes taut then slack,
son-of-a-bitch, hornpout, pumpkinseed.
He's talking to me, or a son he's lost
to this wide country, its wars—
or he doesn't have a son,
just the good fight with a pickerel,
the clunk of an oarlock,
the splash of an oar.

III

Summer Vacations

We're told it's dark and to stick close,
that razors are blue inside taffy apples,
that salt water draws us toward it
needing the light from our young bodies.
In the windshield beyond my parents
milkweed disperses.
And when my fingers move across their backs
they rediscover my St. Vitus' Dance,
the movement of blood in my veins.

I wanted to make a ghost appear at the end
of my story
in the shape of an overcoat.
But no one has died in my family.
I mourn them and my father knows this
and he knows the roller coaster on the night sky
is the shipwreck's scroll
and sees the ocean pearl in the yellow light
from the ferris wheel
as each arcs and arcs again
like the dawns.

Each time my brother switches the channel
I hear the crash of waves, the whales' sad trumpeting.

Wouldn't it for once be possible to get a glimpse of the sea?
I remember hearing the tutor:
Pourquoi vous? L'argent, l'arbre,
the empirical fact
that the small intestine if extended outside the body

reaches my grandmother's bed of azaleas.
I don't want to hold so much in.
First the bed with the brace
like a corral
and the honeycombs threaded with life

behind the cottage.
I keep stories rolled up like sleeping bags
for strangers who stop along the highway,
suddenly afraid. As for the stars
they are there long after the evening's over,
cars gone.

I think of two chairs set off under some trees.
They are never occupied.
I walk a little way there.
The air is wet, the grass.
The mosquitoes float down on a wrist or elbow.
There is no staying here,
other journeys, other fathers.
Over the charcoal embers they stir up a flame or two
into the greater misunderstandings of light and shadow.

Winter, the Dark Hutch

Today I thought about that winter in the birch woods

      of Cape Cod.
A quaint house & not mine

     as all houses aren't—
a two-story condo with a red rabbit hutch.
My friend's father broke the neck of one full grown

       with the back of his hand,
but what bothered me today as hail kept interrupting
my train of thought with its resemblance to corn kernels
bursting in grease & with my tangential association
to the hot smell of butter or margarine

or the dark cinemas in which Lawrence of Arabia goes mad,

what bothered me today here in the damp gulf plains
was the sound of my friend's contraption smoothing beach
   stones
down to bright red & blue folk amulets,

how all night in my sleep the stones churned in their
   chamber
like the sound of the future, like the white

      tremulous bodies in the dark hutch,
which, back then, I wouldn't have bet on—

not that I was cynical, which I was, not that I was fatalistic,
which I was, not that I would give you one big drop
of blood from the neck of a white rabbit

for the future, but that, as my mother says,
      'when it comes it comes.'
I am falling through it whether or not
I give it the nod. My nod

is like the rabbit's when a man's backhand swings down
from the light in the birches.

As I look back through time drenched in all its other
peculiarities, blood beads up on the tar-lacquered tree-stump
        behind the hutch.

For all I know
the birches have slipped off the sleeves of white bark
my friend & I would launch as Viking Ships.

Thor was his dog bounding through the thin ice
appearing just then on the twilit brook
in a desolate resort town
in a country in love with work.
Thor splashed belly down on our fleet,
then shook his matted pelt to mist.

Soon my friend's father would pull up in the drive,
emptying the mailbox, one bill, then the next,
reviling himself with words we loved for the sounds
of the explosive f's & k's, the b's & p's
bursting off his lips.

Would he go mad from money worries, a man
in essence, like any skin of ice on a brook,

no different from the next guy: saliva on the wheel
of the car in rush-hour humiliation, the shimmer of engine
        heat
inside his eyes.

I sometimes wonder where my friend is now.

His name is *Carl Johnson.*

Does he own a house on stilts overlooking a bay,
his wife a quiet sort of saint?

The joke was
that Chastity, Prudence & Security were his sisters,

that his tales of the whispering of nylons on the tub
                    were just so much
baloney, Carl married to the five sisters of his right hand
like most of us all through junior varsity

and senior break. Sometimes the sound of Carl's contraption

is the masculine swagger of branches in a stiff breeze.
When the swift light from the trees sweeps down
across the back of my neck,

I doubt virility will measure up to that moment when the thin
ice of childhood disappears. I was about to say "breaks"

to be dramatic, like Carl's father's backhand,

though that, I'm afraid—for each humming furry heart—
is true as only happenstance is,

swift & out of our hands.

I went away. The thin ice went away. A routine check-up
took Carl's father the following summer.

I remember the open grave,
a green velvet carelessly tossed over the damp earth & clay.

Often in the morning while I listen to my neighbor
warm up his blue sedan, or when I read a book at the
            laundromat,

and from time to time take note of the noise my thick blue
            socks make
leaping in defeated circles inside the dryer,

I think of Carl,
and since I've allowed correspondence to peter out,

I think I must be the rumble & purr of beach stones
at night on the desk in his otherwise silent room.

I lull his head to the pillow. I hold up
his blank meaningless hours of dream.

I wake him at the window streaked with birches,
in a house that isn't his.

The Doctor & the Young Groom

> Well, sir, suspecting that the flood on the Irtish had been
> dreamed up expressly to avoid driving through mud at night, I
> protested and gave orders to go on . . . Off we went. Mud, rain, a
> furious wind, cold . . . and felt boots on.
> It is a long, long trip across the river . . . one long agony!
> —Anton Pavlovich Chekhov

In the distance the tops of trees
look like bristles
on the shaved heads of sailors at Yalta.
Several men, peasant grooms,
as sullen as they are, heave wheels from mud,
water over the axle, the doctor's boots
cold gelatin, cold jelly.
One of the horses veers its whole

blue body, an arc of flood,
a boy going under.

Seal the mouth of the victim with yours.

The boy wakes to the blue ticking of a fire
as the flood goes on with its desire
to fill everything with itself,
which is nothing, all the human veers from—
rain driving against the black cabin door.
The boy remembers his mother's hand
on his forehead,
a hand tracing features on an older face.

Ten fingers boost him among Botticellian pears.

A voice reprimands like a pointer
making sense on a blackboard.

He lofts the pears.
Keep your worm-eaten rocks.
When will the words

thud on the ground at his feet?

*

The cattails are cracked & yellow
like the legs of so many dead shore birds.
On horseback, the young groom in a fur vest

bends down to kiss the brim of the doctor's cap.

Later, the boy draws yams from the earth.
What's this? A parsnip, huge albino root
deep in the ground all winter. It's good luck,
sinewy & sweet as a girl's wrist
across a violin eking out
a quiet music on catgut strings.

*

The doctor remembers the ferry,
his cold feet, the coffee on board a vile soup.
Since his arrival

he's gotten as far as the dry piles of the dock.
Two men are chewing pieces of black bread.
Inside, a woman sits, beaten brass coins
pinning her ears back.

He warms her feet.
From his bag a shaving brush spills
with the black snake of his trade: the stethoscope.
Her heart slowly beats.
Frostbite stings each painted toenail
like the sting of each typewriter key late at night.
No, the pain is nothing like that.
Her bastards offer
a hard green pear.

*

The young groom owes no one a drop.

His fingernails are black ridges
scooping into pails the still-warm sawdust
of horse manure. When it cools
he strews it on the ground.

The red-veined leaves of the beet
blossom, devil's work he thinks, any good
coming so easily into his hands.

The pale ankles of the woman turning at the edge
of the orchard
are nothing like the white fetlocks
of a horse.
He yanks the bit
and the horse makes a sound no horse makes,
the sun a gray pallor behind the sky.

The water rises.

*

Dreaming this, he's a white shirt in a pear tree.

A young woman drops through childhood—thin ice—
skate blades jabbing her, the cattails
she grabs uprooting in her hands
like the straw pulled from old dolls.

Behind a shed, beneath years of dead leaves & pruned
brittle rose thorns
he dreams a scythe
and behind him, as at the edge of a stage, is the doctor
kissing him back to life.

If a scythe appears in the branches of a tree,
someone must swing it.

A white shirt presses her body in the wet grass.
What a thing, undulating!
As he lies back she swings the scythe—
it could cut grass, rusted.
It thuds against his forearm,
just misses his head, an ear
wet & stinging, a brown hard burr.

Morning: a white shirt foams
like the chicken parts boiling in the pot.
The maid scolds two cocks fighting in the doorway.

     *

If the good doctor calls up a woman's body
beside a shed,
if the lights in the house are dusty ash,
does he hear her weeping into her white hands?
If a voice goes out only to disperse, a sip for the ears,
a cat's ghostly cry,
then the doctor is revising a sentence: *the cattails*
are broken & scattered on the road like the legs
of dead herons, like he scoffs
the pens stabbed into a blotter
beneath a ring of light from a lamp.

Today, he thinks, I lanced a Custom Officer's boil.
I had to laugh, blood dribbling down the buttocks
like the vile borscht the Tartars stew in pots
under the wet black trunks of winter trees.

The cat flies up the stairs:
the trill of a calliope.

The doctor is leaning again over the blue lips
of a boy, a young groom twitching on a cot
like a starfish pocked with sand
at the end of a hook.

Face to face
—two angels—
they hear the sound of rushing water,
a sting in the ears, the sound of pears
dropping to the ground, worm-eaten.
A kiss is sealing their lips
with a sound horses never make.

The Umbrella

Seeing an umbrella making its way down the rainy street

the terrible need to sleep and stop seeing people
seems to want to draw near.

In the dream totally myself as though someone else were
        dreaming
I had to change.
I couldn't even catch my breath in the railway station,
the loudspeaker calling out names of towns
in the southern mountains Freilassing, Berchtesgaden . . .

as I heaved my pack from the moving train, the wet snow
brightening the streetlights, the station lights,
just when I wished to creep away unnoticed.

These moments my wife and I are nothing, separate.
Nothing matters but her flank lathering and painful like a
        horse's:
the light on it
taking it away and glistening.

In my lifetime America will sing
the song of the dog's bone.
A lazy trigger finger perches in the limbs
of the chinaberry.
Some nights he's bored with the haze of the moon,
the dust of the road rising to meet it,
his breath—and he sings to my wife by the front porch.
All is old before his eyes and vast.

On my side of the world I feel sometimes as though
I were never born and then a chain rings on the pavement
as a truck roars past on its way to the quarry
where I go at night because the drainage
is metallic blue and the iridescence
of the grackles gliding across the moonlit surface
says accepting life is incredible.

Or maybe I'm making up the details of my life
as I go along,
as it goes along, mistaken perceptions.
I'm stepping down into apples of smoke
right on schedule. Punctual Germans trains!
I'm rushing forward . . . wasting precious hours
sitting in a Japanese garden where rock walls
swirl in an aerial mosaic, and I diminish in a yellow light,
how terrible to be the crest of a hill, an animal
discovering its face.

Land's End

I must be old
when I drive all night to the sea
then don't lie by it.
Sometimes you have to be older than the sea,
you have to be hard, lusterless
and hard. The waves always
curl out of themselves
to the same thing.
In the Portuguese deli
a woman with five snail rings
is slicing a long vein
of linguica.
She's quiet or softly hums
and I love her because she knows
she could never walk out
of her life into mine.

Once on an island
near Venice,
in an abandoned warehouse
or plane hangar that was
the whole island, I saw
the glass blower loop the red-hot
string of glass into a countenance
he said was his mother's.
It was his.
It's this woman's, now,
in this deli near the sea
as I shade my eyes from the glare
off the water.

A boy behind the counter
is going on about a whale
beached off Sunken Meadow.
Maybe it was bored with the swelling
and unswelling tides.

I don't know.
I watch it dying.
The flukes toss lightly in the air
then curl under, drawing sand.
A hairy mouth gaps
below a single gray eye
that doesn't have to look.
Later, police with yellow megaphones
cordon off where fishermen
hose down long pink rolls of blubber
on the back of a truck.
I'll have nothing
to do with the sea.
I lift my eyes to it.

The Hummingbird

—to Isaac Babel

Inside the frame of the mirror
she is nude,
not an embarrassed naked body seen from the window.
Beyond the face in the mirror
is the inner life
stunned by those who again & again
kill your grandfather,
stuffing a writhing fish in his fly.
There's a hummingbird
dipping its beak in nine tiny trumpet blossoms
winding their way up the glass.
It is the kingdom of nectar
and it is this world.

Your secrecy saved you, Isaac.
The pseudonyms.
The secret hide-outs.
Once from a small farmhouse
you watched the lovely brooding edge
of nettles as a boy fell
chasing a sheepdog. He's so nearly you
your mouth fills with the surprise of stinging nettles.
You can't go running through fields
or kissing girls.

A hat slanted on her head,
the woman knows what dipping beneath the surface
of elegant prose has in store
for the burrowing Jewish boy
she senses behind her in the mirror
now that he's gone. In a small room
his secret chest of papers—
Red Cavalry, Old Odessa, "You Must Know
Everything"—overflows.

In one of the stories, women, naked to the waist,
nurse orphaned newborns.
Isaac, the women are waiting for you
to make them live.
A cry issues from a shriveled eggplant
of an infant
on the crook of an arm.

It is not your voice.

The sweet trajectory of hummingbird is vertigo.

*

Hummingbirds love sugar water
my lover says.
Don't feed them honey,
it will kill them.
She unbuttons her dark blouse
and unhooks her bra.

Her landscape of breasts is like milk
with two dark coins floating in it.
Though a man may think of smoke
rising from the tip of a cigarette
over two dark coins at the bottom of a glass
as all the precision he can muster,
as his last chance,
it isn't fear,

it isn't elegy that colors everything
so undependably.
Outside the cannery
children are singing a song their parents sang
when they were children.
Isaac Babel, Isaac Babel,
where are you, you little four-eyes?
Isaac Babel, Isaac Babel,
how does it feel to be alive?
I did not mean to touch the breasts.

I touched them softly as if they were not there
beating wings beneath my hands.
Cuban Emerald, Ruby Throat,
Rufous Hummingbird.
I search for you everywhere.
I wedge a piece of cheese
in the branches of a tree.
I don't know which one, one must be careful.
Hummingbirds love sugar water.
I've wedged a piece of cheese
between two crackers
to dip in your borscht,
to finish this way: two fingers
touching a breast, something on the blurred
bright arc of hummingbird.

               *

This is the dove a man smashed dead
on your forehead.
This is the shrill sound of his voice: *Jew.*
These are the soldiers who hurt the air,
the snowcrust giving way beneath the cadence
of their boots. As you lean over a bowl
of something warm, steam fogs your spectacles.
The soldiers force the door,
they crack the mirror with the butt
of a rifle. You dip past the low branches & shadows,
one feather floating down.

A few days in spring
you flash blue or green,
a visitation:
across the field of stinging nettles,
across a boy's vacant scream,
beneath the distant smoke of the cannery
near the river. You feel everything
going on as before.

The men douse the dark bodies of the salmon.
They lob the entrails to the cats.
The fish are delicious
with a squeeze of lemon.
If you can get a lemon.
If at this time of year
and with considerable resources
you get your hands on one.
A lemon! Tiny eclipse.
A hummingbird whirring.
Eyelashes brush your cheek
as she kisses you.
At the barracks during drills
the recruits shout out before they, too,
gambol in the fields.

Constellation

—to Glenn

Sometimes when the Tucson sky is clear
after a rain I walk out under it
and point out Cassiopeia's zigzag walk,
the Twins curved away from each other
in some dark rich bed of company
spreading a thin light of gossip between them.
Up in the left lower-hand quadrant
the Bear rises from its cave.
In Massachusetts, lost to yourself in a yard of hay,
you scythe till you scythe the gleam
of the curved blade as the last arguments
flash from under where all days
seem to roll down to sleep
to hold such solitude, to let it go.

Here tonight in Arizona the skin doesn't chill
when the night shadows lay their hands
on me. Cardinals—one brownish red,
one bright small wisp of sunset—
flit from trunk to wavering branch,
they're smudges of blood some past revives
to every last detail, the way one's features
screwed up in rage or stupidity are still the child's face
we're born with, though worn to the texture of salt
we can't shake off like salt.
It's a part we throw ourselves into
too completely, the face

widening between us. We forget
the lines the emotion becomes clear along
and the emotion, widening, holds us
like crickets scritching, or the hush
where we've arrived & been, the past

keeping us company. I shinny up a tree
on your father's land to pluck the last
huge blossoms falling to a ground
which closes on itself, a rollercoasting
green on green, a "glen" you name it
after yourself, laughing, as you strike a match
to a shot of whiskey, tossing it down
and, tottering, heave a fiery glass
at a big overhanging pear.

The streak of light—firefly or falling star—
is what gets stuck in the dark,
the heartfelt half-drunk moments
we said what we felt.
Overhead the desert stars more than details
are small textured cubes of salt
darker than the thoughts bobbing my head,
darker than the sky we're forever naming
constellation by constellation.
They never change, it's only what fisheye
lens we see from into what we'll never own,
those bright flames of whiskey,
those downed shots going right to our heads
where they will die.

So Swiftly Past

After patches of high-speed brush, broom
and tumbleweed, paths beaten brown
and once I swear & will swear
as long as I have to to forget
a family living in a shipping box
out of the sun's rays packed in our windshield
that pushes that pain at least so it can't
hold us we go so swiftly past. After miles
of high-rise & low buffeted light

we pull over, thirsty, & two Mexican boys
in a park are smashing a papier-mâché
donkey suspended between two ponderosa
pines. Later, they drag cigarettes from their lips,
breathing on us the ghoulish monotony
of lives we can't change. The Rent-A-Car's
clown-yellow brilliance, like the whorl
of a fingerprint. What would they

do with lives so full of time it's on our hands
like flour?

Kids like time-lapse growths
stitch the landscape descending on us.
A few quicker little ones, gnat-like,
kiss our palms empty, open & white.

                *

Beyond the pavilion, the park's stock
of exotic birds: flapping wings
and webbed feet beat the water to a froth
as a woman scatters the stars of bread more evenly,
having discovered the white centers, weightless,
falling to a few larger birds, the long
neck of a gander or a swan.

74

Some crusts like boats slip out on the water
to carp perforating the surface.
What kind of mind is this that anneals
what it can't change, letting it deliquesce
like leaf mold into millions of tiny colonies
of feeding, all from the idea of a drop of water
like an arrowhead on someone else's
tongue, the sight of us a wonder
at this moment that flaps like a fish
in a pail, white fish, white dock.
Ourselves on the hood of the car,
eating a lunch of bologna & mustard sandwiches
under a sky so bright it sets its table
for everyone & no one, starless & smooth.

*

Our own time, we waste it with topics
of art & normal conversation
and whatever we want. We don't have to choose
or eat. Our mission has chosen
not to let us in on it. We watch
the sun dip, the sky a scratched cornea,
the air a chill that stirs
oblivious to bodies on the grass
drenched with night dew as the swans
bored with curled empty palms
curl into question marks.
If the swan's perspective is lucid
because dumb, the selves we are
call us apart during the night
to pee in some exotic flower's
black & orange center,
to look back at the other's shallow sleep
with the breathlessness of muscles
still believing they're going 60,
70 miles an hour.

The door of the car is open, the measly
interior light: as though we wished it all:
the car, the travelers' cheques in the glovey,
the green face of a digital wristwatch, some
love we can't afford ourselves,
wished it all would go away
in dark empty hands wanting most of all
what makes us live.

Street Noises

Across the street, out of the bed of a pick-up
a Mexican worker flings bricks two at a time

to a man balancing himself on a sandpile, to one
on a scaffold, to another higher up. How quickly

my own abrupt sentences wind around themselves
like mating snakes, how Aesculapius' serpentine

arms must have ached healing so much. One man
keeps a beat as he smoothes mortar with a trowel

and slices an edge, warbling some top-forty tune
to call just the right measure of attention

to himself as a red-tipped sliver of sun
shivers in the wobbly pane of picture window

that two other men are shouldering toward a door
as the glass, too, shoulders the distant amber

we'll soon dissolve into, one poor cloud: barely white.
I listen to the crepe myrtle whine with cicadas

as if moonstruck, bound & strummed with volts,
it won't quiet, won't let me lose myself

to how barely the human body houses its weak
and charred kid-brother: the mind's beautiful

forgetfulness taking us all inside it
and destroying us to keep us. When the men

are done for the day, sawdust blows from sills
and a nail rolls in wind & pings as it falls

hitting something below, some unknown
tuning fork for which silence

is the eager philharmonic: the long-haired
pin-oak virtuosos drawing branch across branch,

a cement mixer the callow never-called-for kettle drum.
Next door, the leaning TV antenna picks up frenzy

in the dust bowl of the air, the chop-chop
drumming of its wand against shingles.

The men do not miss this music, their sinewy
absence has much to do with how the scaffolds

sway a bit in wind from the Gulf.
The morning brings their raucous encore.

A blue jay flares up to a branch, like noon,
driving off a morning fog, a mourning dove's

surreptitious sadness our hearts pick up on,
a sad normal inhalation of air blown out.

Home

Along the freeway a wax cup
circles in wind,
cars zip by snipping houses like postage stamps,
plink, plink, plink,
mad philatelist.
You pull over & from the only
Mexican take-out in South Tucson, this dream island
in America, you watch kids exchange hits of grass.
They hold it in.
A grackle they hear then see
splits seeds like vowels,
its iridescence squeezed through the eye.
The sweet lost opulence
of the eye.

Does it comfort the air it swerves through
when you're home,
the hiss & grind of the garbage truck
shaking the road & taking nothing?
A spaniel two years dead paces the fence
and you see yourself as a young child again.
Dad's two hands, the sun—
your two ass buns two peaches ripening
to stand for awkwardness, a flag.

Now before the hall mirror
your face is a planet
suffering its bodies of water,
the tensing of lineaments like Dad's eyes, Dad's
cleft chin, it isn't portrait
it's escape. Mom's in there
behind the face
the way the roots of the big old elm
endlessly revise the earth.
Why so deeply love?
Addresses escape the mailbox.

Your brother's infant crawls awhile
then wails.
Dad's doing the windows.
With an even-measured smile of thanks, love,
blame, self-blame—
with a familiar splash of gunmetal
water on the sides of the pail
he strops the glass
on the storm door.
The aluminum family L curls its tail,
an omen now that what it stood for
is lost or almost lost
and we are here.